EARTHWORKS

Jacqueline Gabbitas

Stonewood
THUMBPRINTS

First published in 2012
by Stonewood Press
97 Benefield Road, Oundle PE8 4EU
Tel: 0845 456 4838
books@stonewoodpress.co.uk
www.stonewoodpress.co.uk

All rights reserved
Poems © Jacqueline Gabbitas, 2012
The author assert her moral right to be
indentified as the author of this work

ISBN: 978-0-9569122-3-7

Distributed by Central Books
99 Wallis Road, London E9 5LN
Email: orders@centralbooks.com
Tel: 0845 458 9911

Printed and bound in the UK by Imprintdigital, Exeter

Designed and typeset in Minion 10.5pt/12.5pt
by www.silbercow.co.uk
Cover illustration by Martin Parker

This is the first book in the THUMBPRINT series

ACKNOWLEDGEMENTS

Some of the poems in this collection first appeared (some in earlier versions) in the following magazines: 'In Principio' (as 'February') in *Poetry Salzburg Review*, 'Lappen' in *Artemis Poetry*, 'The Padfield Horse' *Staple Magazine*, and 'Overlaid' on the New Writing Ventures Website in 2007. I would like to thank the editors and publishers of all of these. I would also like to thank the Hawthornden Castle Fellowship for my residency in 2009.

I am indebted to Mimi Khalvati for her invaluable support and guidance and Preetha Leela Chockalingham for her evergreen enthusiasm for my work, thank you both. I also thank Stonewood Press for producing a beautiful chapbook, and Sharon Morris for her kind words.

For Martin, with love

CONTENTS

OVERLAID	7
DAMFLASK	8
DEER SHELTER	10
WATER CALTROP	12
HIGH HILLS	13
IN PRINCIPIO	14
BIRD BURIED	16
THE PADFIELD HORSE	18
A SPEEDING HEART	20
APRIL END (BELTANE)	22
I'VE NO SOUL TO TELL YOU ON	23
EPPING FOREST LIZARD	24
LAPPEN	25
WOOD & STONE	26
HANDFAST FIRE	27
SONGS OF COAL	28
SEATEARTH	29
STIGMARIA	30
NOTES AND DEDICATIONS	32

OVERLAID

'You're late.' 'I'm sorry, I overlaid.'
'You overslept?' I overlaid.
I covered myself in sleep:

I lived in the ground not calling it dirt,
I burrowed: the seatearth known as fireclay.

There were bones, cast off shells,
and nothing familiar

until beetles – chitin sticking in my teeth,
shellac, shellac too. And ash
– ash sustained me –
and sediment,
and the damp from ancient mires.

My eyes crusted with salt,
and I welcomed the stinging.
When the heat was too much
I took flint to my hair,
breathed through the gaps in my teeth,
their remnants.

DAMFLASK

Valleys know water and depth, black and cold.
Chub (nipping at mosquitoes and midges) swim
slow and fast here. Deeper down there's twenty-
thirty pound of pike and the sharpest beaks.

We'd come to walk the reservoir; come at dusk
to see the heron in flight, the horseshoe bats
(and one solitary bat flitted like a swallow,
uncaring of our presence beneath its food path).

But the level of water alarmed us – they call it
hochwasser in Germany as if it's a holy thing.
Nests in the embanked trees were almost pike food,
and anything below them crazed. Broken.

We learned later that the *hochwasser* was higher
than it had been over a century ago, when Damflask
(village and people) had been crushed under
the Great Inundation – bodies bloated and rotting.

We learned how miles down stream, mothers,
husbands, colleagues, babies, were identified
and carted back to be claimed and collected
before the season's heat took them to the flies.

Yet skirting Damflask then, we carried with us
only recent headlines where 'man swept away
by floodwater' had the weight of stocks falling,
until a man walking his dog stopped us to talk.

DEER SHELTER

What surrounds it is a dry-stone wall, low
and heartened with the death of stones
re-born as a gathering of strength.

The wall contains a station, also stone,
and that contains the ghosts of wild deer
who gathered for safety, and later were killed.

The meat of the deer's leaner than that of the lamb.

And deer need deer just as we need each other.
They'd gather in the station and find shelter
from sky – from the terror, the miracles, it brings.

Lives have been lived since then.
Now the shelter's a space re-born for sky,
marshalling in the ever-changing light.

I'm on my back, in pain, watching clouds,
the ache of rooks, and a dozen sea birds
heading out to ports, landfills or wetlands.

On her own, a child enters and stares up.
I'm no threat then, this woman
sleeping in the corner with both eyes open.

And neither is the girl. But she has power,
in the centre of her infant heart – a quiet –
and for a moment we're transformed:

she, with the mouth and eyes of St Giles,
me with the trembling of the saint's small deer,
and my pain is a king's arrow aimed to kill.

The meat of the deer's leaner than that of the lamb.

WATER CALTROP

Eat of it. Peel its newly boiled skin and eat and do well.
Do not consume it raw for it carries the fluke. Thin worm.

Worm with teeth. This caltrop is waternut, its shell
black, striated and dazzling in this light, this autumn.

Boil and eat of it. Nourish the blood, the expectant swell
of heart, brain, sinew. Find it in a river resting on a berm.

Worship it, for it has been worshipped – Flesh Bull,
Bull God – horn made of plant, in its meat all symbol.

This caltrop brings down no tanks, camels, war-elephants,
just fevers and ills in all their consumptive, sweating forms.

Know of it and it will protect you. Find it or buy it,
but call it by its name, *ling jiao*, and make of it an amulet.

HIGH HILLS

See how the skies drag blue over grey.
We're sick and only the hills have a cure
and always the centre is flint, is clay.

But this is a day like any other day –
feel the step of moorland or forest floors,
see how the skies drag blue over grey.

The hills beneath us will have their say:
*We can resist what your bodies endure,
and always, the centre is flint, is clay.*

But pain is a measure, living a delay:
These hills, they promise nothing for sure.
See? How the *skies* drag blue over grey.
And *always* the centre is flint, is clay.

IN PRINCIPIO

She looks for the cold places;
the wintered flesh where the naked
shoulder meets the neck. She holds

a hand against them, draws up
what cold she can, leans against surfaces;
tiled, glazed.

And time, as it should, passes.

Passes, as she sees herself
walking in snow, covered in furs: fur
around wrists, fur lining her hood.

Her boots on slow ground. She holds

her hands longer than is safe in rivers,
streams, (where even frogs have evacuated,
fish hibernate), holds them
until the little fingers turn grey,

then she slips them between her legs, where
she knows the body's warmest, and asks
the small questions: *Are you here,*

*or am I imagining you? Is the air
so thin I can't stand it? Tell me,
am I* floundering? *And tell me,*

*when your body hit the cremation fire
what happened? Did they both release a hiss;
one of welcome, one goodbye?*

BIRD BURIED

I pick it up by a foot, its arthritic
claws missing a talon, lower it in,
shovel soil, and put a brick on top.

It's not a marker I say, knowing
already that's a lie. I tell myself
its to stop the foxes scavenging,

but it's the base of a cairn,
and tomorrow I'll most likely add
another stone from the garden.

The ground, wet from days of rain,
sticks to the trowel like tar. But
this is a garden, so *ground* is *soil*.

And beneath this brick
is a passing place where *soil*
becomes *earth* because of death.

And the bird, missing its talon,
has a human burial, albeit
without the words or any of the songs.

I set to weeding the kale beds,
the bulb fennel – no tubers,
nothing underground except radish

and that's already bolted. I hum,
a habit learned while still a child –
give the world its distance,

if only for the length of a chorus –
and in the treeline the sparrows sing,
their lungs small, almost bursting.

THE PADFIELD HORSE

My stomach was full of half-digested
food, not quite enjoyed but eaten
for needing food, and I had beer
too, enough to keep me warm.

I tell you this, so you can imagine
the moment when crossing a field
stile after stile, Martin stops, silent,
says, 'That's a horse.' It is white.

I have no night-vision; the horse,
standing as still as it can – its ears
flicking, turning; nostrils enlargening –
enfleshes before us. Becomes.

If I'd been alone, I might have
missed it or might have thought
it was one of your horses – the ones
from your book – but instead

Martin and I crept to the fence,
which was also white, and offered
the one offering we had – a handful
of Austrian pumpkin seeds.

And that should have been it, except
one image endured: Two pilgrims
crossing a thin path marked out
by leylines, the sky dulled by smoke

from the village bonfires, to greet
a horse borne out of darkness
to materialize for them, its ears
twitching to the hymns of fireworks.

But we were not these pilgrims,
we were in awe, yes, but drunk too
and unprepared for feeding horses,
and unprepared for its soft rejection.

A SPEEDING HEART

Nothing of love in it, but the rush
of blood and adrenaline, holding a breath,
gone, held, gone – and
the heart
speeding like a car in a waltzer.
I felt it in my throat,
like we do, we do
on exertion, when we've pushed
and pushed, or been pushed
until the only thing we can do
is let it out of our mouths into the air, gagging
as we gag. The heart
gasping for its life, unsupported by us,
no longer supporting us,
free of the tissue, veins,
the arteries that make it ours,
astonished in its freedom –
in how
it squeezed between our lips,
scraped against the backs of our teeth,
our hind-teeth scoring lines like staves
on its thickened flesh.

No longer our music
– a rhythm quiet in us – the heart's
rapidity is heard over the skies,
through the walls,
the rails of the underground:
the heart, the heart,
the heart, the heart, the heart. Has
wings, propulsion, has
vision in its sightless muscle.

APRIL END (Beltane)

This is the fire sermon:
a thousand believers, half-
believers and *fire will raise dead ground*.

Drum is the firesong. Drum and silence.
And waiting on cracked seed and shells.
Waiting on sky. And here

in the fire sermon, half-naked
on hill marked sacred by whisky,
fire and song, he gives her stone (flint

made passive by rain, earth, Gods).
Frog-stone, a gem for her open pocket.
A jewel for this newest day.

I'VE NO SOUL TO TELL YOU ON

I've no soul to tell you on. No soul, no earth.
Minerals grate in mi teeth. I've a nail's worth
o' iron in mi blood, an' gold – enough to mek
your eyes ret keen, an' any's enough to tek.

There's no earth in mi blood. An' so I eat
till there's none left beneath mi feet.
If I 'old up this 'and, 'n' this 'un, what's there?
But t'smell o'soap, an' this scar 'ere,

an' this 'un, an' this 'un? And yet in one 'and
I've 'andful o'clay, t'other loam, but no soul,
no, just t'slow, steady grate an' grind o' 'om'.
If there's glass in this clay – loam fine as sand –
if there's reason to question what's true an' loyal,
then I've no earth to love, no soul to tell you on.

EPPING FOREST LIZARD

In the light, the lizard is less than it should be.
When it moves and wrong-foots us, we make noises
to show how wrong-footed we are.

My memory of lizards is islanded on coastal walls,
their tiny outlines logos for something quiet,
ready for the second when you blink in the sun –

– or it's from Texas and the small way
they'd wait in the shade of trees scattered
across deserts bracketing the tarmac roads.

This lizard has stopped again (it could be plastic).
It has no movement to give us, no startled fear –
it's not like the roe deer we stumbled upon,

or like the squirrels, once killed and eaten
by thin-soled men with sling-shots and dogs,
(quiet men who set the trees as forest over wood),

and its actions feel true; as if it's the one honest thing
in this place of garrets and asylums, of dappled light
that even now wrong-foots me in its memory.

LAPPEN

Brings to mind the hare, eyes goat-like;
the dog, ears pointing stiff;
brings up the lapis stone, easily describable –
(not like Blue John, whose purpled veins
is the blood of those who live above
its worked-out seams). *Lappen!*
Oh, a rag, a cloth, a scrap, a sop
for history and words, a wipe
for dust and soap – it's not a flannel

though it's disguised to be: an old
cotton underskirt ripped into squares,
a pair of knickers in a bath. We called it
flannel, but *Lappen* is truer; if we'd had it
we would have used the word.

So, keep your flannel,
your perfect carded square, give me
the hare to run against, the dog
to care for me, the stone perfect on my throat.
Give me the scrap and rag. By now, I have its shape.

WOOD & STONE

I'll wock in wood, then, an' steown. I'll know
this that's 'ard'll be med soft, redooced
to shavin's o' alabaster and a thin, fine core.

And this 'un that's soft, it'll be softer under
steam an' t'plane. Be bent way I bend mi spine
at t'stooping of a word I caahn't 'ear.

Steown between mi finger an' thumb, is it neowt
but a pebble? An' this in t'palm o' mi hand
a cobble? An' this 'un ont'flooer between one
knee and tuther, only a boulder?

An' this tree, this cracking bit o' ash,
stripped onit's bark an' planed an' planed,
I could mek flooers wi' it. But this is Tree –
unstripped, where there's things still live in it.

HANDFAST FIRE

Some choose a besom;
                      a grass fire is best.

Leap its height

– even though it's dug into a pit
its heat
       is higher
              than the level of a heart,
                          it reaches
                              almost
to the shoulders,
burns
       both names into the skin.

This fire draws its life
              from the stones
              that encircle it,
                        the sun
that warmed them in the day;
draws it
       from those explosions
                      when the tectonic plates shattered
and all the mountains formed.

SONGS OF COAL

Sparks and the blunting of your blade.
Moss is collected, bark stripped
off the silverest of birches.

Call me peat. I give you the flame,
small and fuelled. You smell it
as it burns even this earth.

*

Remember that first giving:
its warmth carried in your hands,
strapped to your back, a rough cart.

You tunnel now; strip carbon black
from brown. Call me anthracite.
Ready me here for excavation.

Control your explosions – a network,
diamonding the seam in which I *am*.
Remember the giving.

And you, you find a safe place.
Detonate. A spark, explosion. Rock
splinters and falls. Set me aside.

SEATEARTH

Nothing but clay –
beneath these clothes is skin
skin tissue
tissue bones
– and clay is marrow;

nothing but clay
and heat and heart
and earth
and hearth.

Cherishing bones
borne into limestone
– elephants and hyena –
tusk or shin, claw or incisor.

Cherishing words
full in the mouth
– warrant, root clay –
the casts of heart muscles,
the lycopod stigmaria.

STIGMARIA

It's there always, a kind of reassurance,
this beautiful grey root. It will be lifted,
dusted, placed back with love, a history
of love, a simple needing of its presence,
and looked at everyday. Only the heart
remains of it, became this precious fossil.
Think of the beauty in the once fine crossing
of its rootlets, lost now and calcified as scars.
Think of the crudest breaks where the pressure
of earth was absolute. Think of its resurrection,
and how you hold it resting in your palm
(itself warm and generous in the measure
of tissue, skin and bone), and give protection
to its systolic past, protect its acre of calm.

NOTES AND DEDICATIONS

Deer Shelter   After the artwork *Deer Shelter* by American artist, James Turrell. Yorkshire Sculpture Park, Wakefield.

St. Giles is the patron saint of lepers and the disabled (some include long-term illness in this). He lived in a grotto on the River Rhone, near Arles, France. One day the king was out hunting and shot at the small deer that lived with St. Giles. The saint put out his hand to protect it. The king's arrow pierced St. Giles' hand and the deer was saved.

High Hills   Kaolinite is a white china clay with extensive uses including in ceramics and medicine. It is named after the Chinese high hill Kao-Ling, is one of the most common minerals and is mined across the UK and the world.

In Principio – i.m. June Gabbitas

The Padfield Horse – for Sharon Morris

Epping Forest Lizard – for Preetha

Songs of Coal   Contemporary mining techniques sometimes use controlled explosions in a diamond-shaped grid to release a seam.

Stigmaria – for David and Steven